2HOUR
Treasure Hunt
TM

Congratulations!

You've been selected to join the legendary league
of 2Hour Treasure Hunters!

Our Explorers carry out missions around the world, uncovering the
treasures and secrets around us – and making lasting memories.

Your mission today is to complete the Colonial
New York hunt in New York City, USA.

Follow this guide to find the special locations in Lower
Manhattan and complete each Explorers' Challenge.

As you walk from place to place, you'll have some
highlights from Colonial history and some curious
Explorer facts to read along the way.

- Be alert and stay with your friends. They might spot something you miss.

- Bring something to write with to help complete your challenges.

- Be creative. Make this guide your own. Draw, take notes, color the pages. It's the record of your adventure.

- Be on the lookout for the bonus locations. You never know what you might find around the next corner!

And don't forget to use your imagination! It's your most important gear. No true Explorer would leave home without it!

Let's get started

1 Find your way to the cross streets listed for each location.

2 Once you're there, read about where you are and what happened there.

3 Then take a good look around and complete the Explorers' Challenge.

4 Scan this QR code for directions:

Where are you?

Welcome to New York City! Can you find New York City on a map of the United States of America?

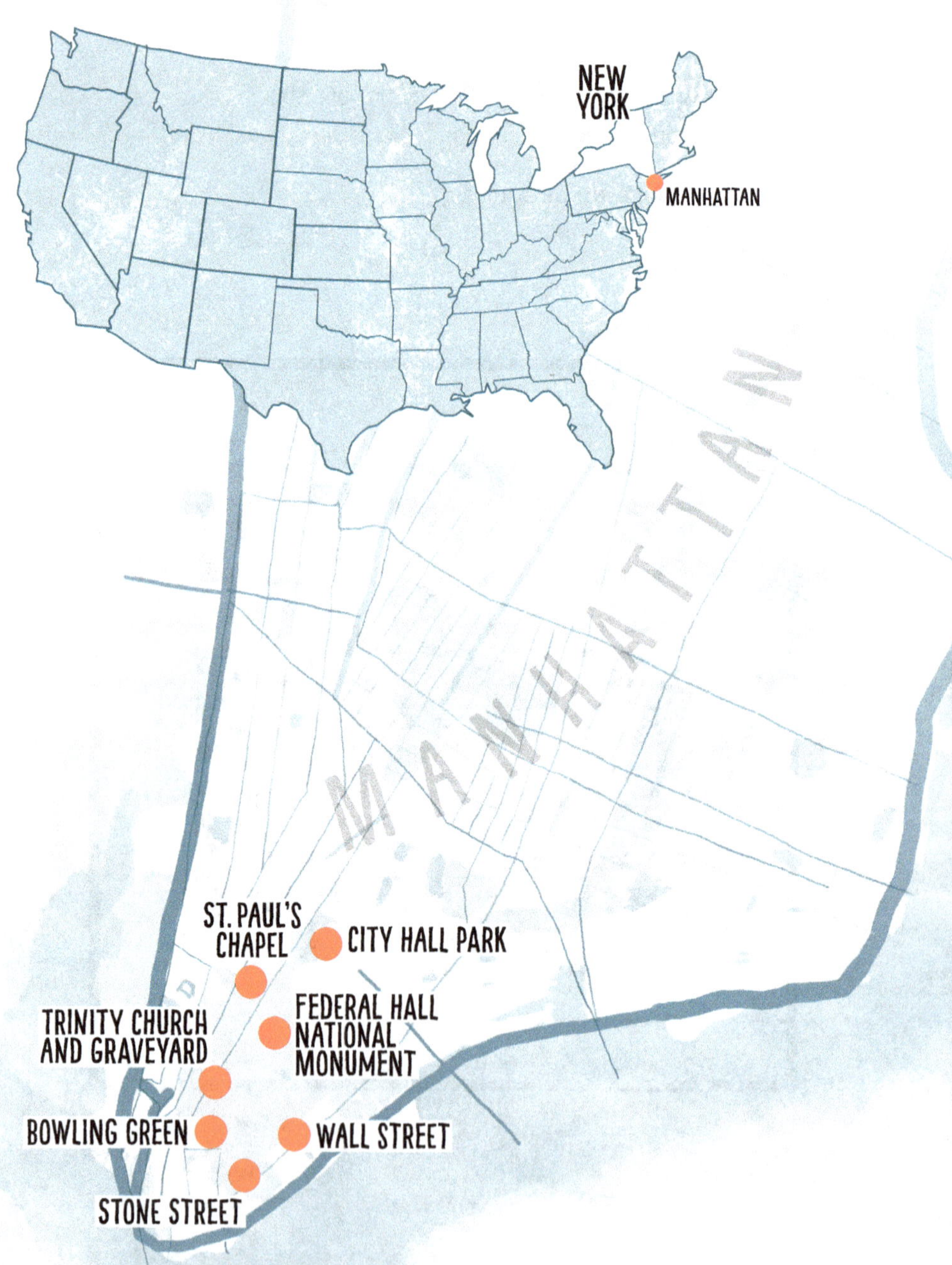

New York City, which is in New York State, is the largest city, based on population size, in the United States of America.

While it's not the capital of New York State, it was once the capital of the newly-formed United States of America.

Long before it became New York, this land was home to the Lenape people, a Native American tribe. They called this island Manahatta, meaning "land of many hills."

The Lenape people lived here for thousands of years, living off the forests, rivers and abundant wildlife. They built small villages, fished the rivers, and traveled by canoes made from tree trunks.

Can you imagine New York City filled with trees instead of buildings?

Today you'll explore a neighborhood and very special time period in New York City's history.

Along the way, you'll learn about life and events that took place in New York during the Colonial period and the American Revolution, American's war for independence from Britain.

Bonus locations

Explorers always need to be on the lookout for new and interesting sites.

Keep an eye out for these locations during your treasure hunt.

Charging Bull

Charging Bull is a bronze sculpture that stands on Broadway, just north of Bowling Green Park. He weighs 7,100 pounds and is 11 feet tall and 16 feet long! He acts as a symbol of financial optimism and prosperity.

Battery Park

Battery Park is named for the cannon defenses built in 1683 and was the site of Fort Amsterdam, later renamed Fort George by the British. At the beginning of the Revolution in 1776, the American revolutionaries fired the cannons at British ships in the harbor from here.

Portal to Old New York

Across the street and up the block from Fraunces tavern is a real window down into old Colonial New York. Here under glass set in the sidewalk, you can find remnants of Colonial-era New York. These were discovered during an archaeological dig.

Statue of Liberty

Seen from a distance between buildings or across Battery Park, the Statue of Liberty stands on Ellis Island. The statue symbolizes freedom and democracy. Did you know that the 305-foot-tall statue was originally a shiny reddish brown, like a new penny? Over time, the copper reacted with the air and the elements, forming the now famous green color.

City Hall Park

In the mid-1700s, New York was a thriving colony under British rule, but not everyone was happy about being a British colony.

The British government put taxes on things like tea, paper, and stamps. But the colonists had no say in the taxes they had to pay or how the taxes would be used.

This upset them because they believed in "no taxation without representation." So, many New Yorkers began to rebel against British rule. By 1776, the American Revolution began. New York was right in the middle of the action. People were excited and ready to fight for freedom.

City Hall Park was the site of one of the most important moments in American history.

Here George Washington – the general who eventually led the American forces to victory in the war and who became the first president of the United States – read the "Declaration of Independence" to the people of New York, just days after it was signed.

The Declaration of Independence was a document written by America's Founding Fathers and agreed to by all 13 colonies. It announced their decision to break free of British rule to form a new, independent country.

Imagine the excitement and anticipation as people gathered here to hear about their new freedom from British rule!

This park has seen many protests, celebrations, and moments of change. It's a place where New Yorkers have always come together to make their voices heard.

Draw a revolutionary flag

Many colonists made their own flags to show their support for independence.

Design your own revolutionary flag. Think about the colors and symbols you might use to represent a call for independence and freedom.

Next location:

Broadway & Fulton Street (2-minute walk)

Explorer facts

- In Colonial times, church bells set the daily schedule – most families did not have a clock or other way of keeping time.

- Colonial houses were small, with big families often sharing one or two rooms.

- Trash collection and street cleaning didn't happen in Colonial New York. So, who did the cleanup? The pigs, of course! Pigs roamed freely and ate the garbage.

St. Paul's Chapel

Built in 1766, St. Paul's Chapel is the oldest surviving church in Manhattan. It even survived the Great Fire of 1776, which destroyed much of New York City during the American Revolution.

George Washington prayed here after his inauguration as the first president of the United States in 1789.

Draw a historic stained-glass window

Many old churches have beautiful stained-glass windows.

Create your own window that shows something important from history – maybe the signing of the United States Constitution or George Washington's first day as president.

Next location:

Broadway & Wall Street (6-minute walk)

Now let's learn about New York's early history as we walk...

Once upon a time

In 1609, the first European ship arrived, captained by Henry Hudson, a Dutch explorer.

He explored what we now call the Hudson River, hoping it would be a shortcut to Asia. (Spoiler alert: It wasn't!)

But this land was perfect for trade. By 1624, the Dutch set up a trading post and named the new settlement New Amsterdam.

At that time, New Amsterdam was tiny compared to modern NYC – just a small fort, some houses, and many muddy streets.

Yet, it was very important because it was great for trading fur with the Native Americans. People came from all over Europe, making it one of the most diverse places in the world, even back then.

In 1664, New Amsterdam became New York when the English arrived and claimed the city. (The English, like the Dutch, named their new settlements after a city back home, in this case, York.)

Even before the Revolution, New York City was a place of change, trade, and diversity.

From the peaceful lands of the Lenape to the bustling streets of New Amsterdam, and finally the city that would play a key role in America's fight for independence, this island has always been a center of activity.

Trinity Church and Graveyard

Did you expect to find a graveyard right in New York City? Trinity Church has been an important part of New York since its founding in 1697. The current church building, completed in 1846, is the third one on this site, after two earlier versions were destroyed.

The church's graveyard is the final resting place for many notable figures from American history.

Find the famous graves

- Take a walk through the graveyard and see what interesting gravestones you can find.

- Find at least three historical figures buried here and learn an interesting fact about each one. Who knows, you might discover a new hero!

Here is a list of people you might find:

Alexander Hamilton

Elizabeth Schuyler

Hercules Mulligan

Horatio Gates

John Jacob

Robert Fulton

William Alexander

Next location:

Wall Street (1-minute walk)

Explorer facts

- Bagels are boiled, not baked. The secret is out! Boiling is what gives New York bagels their chewy texture.

- NYC has the oldest pizza place in America. Lombardi's (in Brooklyn) has been serving slices since 1905!

Wall Street – The Famous Wall

Wall Street wasn't always filled with bankers and tall buildings.

It was named after the defensive wall built by Dutch settlers in the 1600s to protect New Amsterdam from potential attacks by Native Americans, the British, and even pirates!

The wall ran across Manhattan. On one side of the wall, there was a settlement of wooden buildings and on the other side fields and forest.

By 1699 the wall was torn down as the city expanded. Although it is long gone, the name Wall Street reminds us of the early days when New York was just a small colony.

Look closely down the middle of the street. Can you find the spots that show where the original wall stood?

Design your own wall

Take a moment to think about how you'd build a protective wall for New York.

Draw your wall. Would it be tall and strong? Would you have secret passageways for sneak attacks?

What would your wall protect you from?

Next location:

Nassau Street & Pine Street (3-minute walk)

Explorer facts

- Colonial fashion was much more formal than what we wear today. For example, women often wore gowns over petticoats and men wore coats and breeches with tights. Children dressed in miniature versions of adults' clothes.

- In Colonial New York, men wore wigs and powdered them with flour (which mice sometimes had as a snack!).

Federal Hall National Monument

This is where George Washington officially became first president of the United States in 1789.

It was also the first home of Congress and the Supreme Court! It's the birthplace of American government.

Create a new law

Pretend you are a member of the first Congress in 1789.
What new law would you create to make the country better?

Write down your idea and explain why it's important.

Next location:

Broadway & Beaver Street (10-minute walk) + bonus location alert!

Explorer facts

- New Yorkers are fast talkers and fast walkers. It's said New Yorkers walk 1.3 times faster than the average American!

- The Statue of Liberty came in pieces! She arrived from France in 350 separate parts and took 4 months to put together.

Let's learn about life for children in Colonial New York as we walk...

Not all fun and games!

Life as a child in Colonial New York was very different from today. Whether you lived in the busy streets of New York City or out on a farm in the countryside, childhood meant early mornings, daily chores, and learning to grow up fast.

Most kids woke up at sunrise and helped around the house. Boys might fetch water, feed chickens, or help in the workshop, while girls helped cook, sew, or care for younger siblings. There were no video games, but there were wooden toys, marbles, hoops, and lots of outdoor games like tag or hide-and-seek.

Only some children went to school. If you were a boy in the city and your family was wealthy, you might attend a one-room schoolhouse or be taught by a private tutor. Girls were often taught at home, learning to read the Bible and take care of a home. Books were expensive and rare, so students wrote with chalk on slate boards and memorized lessons.

By age 10 or 12, many kids were expected to start apprenticeships, learning a trade like printing, blacksmithing, or weaving. Others worked on farms or helped run family businesses.

Childhood didn't last long and responsibilities started young. Sundays were all about church, and everyone was expected to sit quietly for hours. Holidays, like Christmas or New Year's were big family affairs, with songs, games, and special meals.

Though life could be hard, kids found time for fun and made-up games with whatever they had – sticks, rocks, corn husks, and imagination.

While there were no modern comforts, children in Colonial New York learned skills, stories, and traditions that helped shape the world we live in today.

Want to step into their shoes? Imagine what you would do if you lived in a one-room home without electricity or running water. How would you spend your time?

Bowling Green

Bowling Green is the oldest public park in New York City, originally established in 1733.

It was a site of protests during the build-up to the American Revolution.

In July 1776, after the reading of the Declaration of Independence, patriots pulled down the statue of King George III that stood here and melted parts of it down to make bullets for the war effort.

The iron fence around Bowling Green still has dents where the British crown symbols were torn off by revolutionaries. Can you find them?

Create a new statue

During the American Revolution, the statue of King George III was torn down. Design a new statue to put in its place.

Draw your creation on the next page.

Between Broadway & Broad Street (5-minute walk)
+ bonus location alert (X2)!

Explorer facts

- In Colonial New York, indoor plumbing did not exist. Instead of bathrooms, families used chamber pots, which were bowls or small ceramic buckets, kept under beds or in closets.

- Many people would dump their chamber pots right out the window, often with a shout of "Gardyloo!" (a warning borrowed from the French phrase "regardez l'eau" meaning "watch out for the water"). What if you had to dump your toilet out of the window each morning?

- In some cases, night soil men (basically early sanitation workers) would collect waste and haul it away at night. They'd cart it outside the city or sell it as fertilizer.

- The first modern elevator was installed in NYC. It was in 1857 at 488 Broadway, thanks to its inventor Mr. Elisha Otis.

Stone Street

Stone Street is one of New York's oldest streets. It was made of two 17th-century roads from the Dutch colony of New Amsterdam:

- Brower Straet – which meant brewers street, named for the breweries that originally lined the street

- Hoogh Straet – which meant high street

In 1658 it became the first cobbled street in New Amsterdam.

Imagine the past

Walk the cobblestones of the street and look around.

Stop and close your eyes. Imagine what the city looked like when Stone Street was first built. Write down three things you might see, hear or smell here.

Next location:

Pearl Street & Broad Street (5-minute walk) + bonus location alert!

Explorer facts

- In Colonial New York, horses and carriages were essential for transportation – but they weren't just parked on the streets like modern cars. Some inns, taverns, and wealthy families had small private stables, called carriage houses.

- Livery stables were like Colonial parking garages. People could rent a horse or carriage or board their own there if they lived in an apartment or small house. These stables were often located near taverns, markets, and ferry landings. Travelers arriving by ship or carriage could drop off their horse for care and feeding.

- Colonial New York cuisine was a mix of English, Dutch and Caribbean influences. Common dishes included fresh oysters from New York harbor, pigeon and other meat pies, salted or pickled fish, and stews of root vegetables like turnips, carrots and potatoes.

Fraunces Tavern

A colonial tavern was so much more than just a place to eat and drink – it was the social heart of a town in the 1600s and 1700s. Think of it as part restaurant, part inn, part post office, part town hall, and part gossip hub, all rolled into one rustic, candlelit building.

Fraunces Tavern was a key meeting place during the American Revolution and is one of New York's oldest buildings, dating back to 1719.

Samuel Fraunces, a tavern keeper of African and French descent, opened the tavern, which was the frequent location for the Culper Ring's secret meetings and spy activities during the Revolution.

It became famous when George Washington said goodbye to his troops here after the end of the war. It is rumored that George Washington's favorite meal, chicken pot pie, was often served here – and it still is today!

The Culper Ring used coded messages printed in newspapers and invisible ink to send and receive information. The Culper Ring code book used the code 727 for New York. Men and women were members. The identity of one of the best-known members, who was a woman called Agent 355, is still a mystery today.

Craft a secret code

Craft your own code and write a message to send secretly.

Below you'll find two ciphers (a simple alphabet code) with practice codes.

Crack the codes to find a secret message George Washington could have sent!

Cipher:

A:Z   B:Y   C:X   D:W   E:V   F:U   G:T
H:S   I:R   J:Q   K:P   L:O   M:N

How to decode:

1. Find each letter pair on the left (A–M) or right (N–Z).
2. Replace it with the letter directly opposite it (AZ, ZA, BY, YB, etc.).

Practice codes:

Cipher: SVOOL

HINT: A friendly greeting

Cipher: ZWEVMGFIV ZDZRGH

HINT: Something brave and exciting – and then something that happens soon

Answer key (Don't peek until you try!):

- SVOOL **HELLO**

- ZWEVMGFIV ZDZRGH **ADVENTURE AWAITS**

Now create your own cipher and coded message for your fellow explorers to solve.

Your cipher

A:	B:	C:	D:
E:	F:	G:	H:
I:	J:	K:	L:
M:	N:	O:	P:
Q:	R:	S:	T:
U:	V:	W:	X:
Y:	Z:		

Your secret message:

- In the 1700s, there were over 18 languages spoken in NYC. Today, there are over 800 languages spoken here. It's the most linguistically diverse city on Earth!

Onward!

Congratulations, Explorers! You've completed today's hunt!

You've followed secret trails, solved puzzling codes, and uncovered stories hidden in stone walls, churchyards, and taverns.

Along the way, you've walked in the footsteps of sailors, shopkeepers, generals, spies and everyday colonists who once called this city home.

Like true explorers you didn't just look – you discovered.

You learned how a wall once gave its people protection and a street its name. You traced the echoes of freedom at Federal Hall. You stood where revolution brewed at Fraunces Tavern and uncovered how Bowling Green's iron fence still bears the marks of a toppled king.

You proved that every brick, plaque, and corner can whisper a story if an explorer is curious enough to pay attention.

The streets of Colonial New York are yours to remember, and the world beyond is waiting for you to explore!

Speak like a New Yorker

The Big Apple is where words move as fast as taxis and every neighborhood has its own slang.

New Yorkers are proud, direct, and full of expression.

English	How a New Yorker might say it	Meaning / when to use it
Hello	How ya doin'?	Friendly, casual greeting (often said fast – "howyadoin")
Goodbye	A'right, see ya	Quick and cool way to say goodbye
Coffee	Caw-fee	It's the city's favorite drink – pronou nced with that classic NY accent
You all	You guys / yous	How some New Yorkers address a group
Traffic jam	Gridlock	When the streets are totally packed
Corner store	Bodega	Small neighborhood shop for snacks and drinks
Pizza	Slice	"Gimme a slice" = "I'd like a piece of pizza"
Metro / underground	Subway / "the train"	The underground train system / "I'm takin' the train uptown" – even if it's underground

- Say "Hey, how ya doin'?" when you walk into a shop.

- Order a 'slice' or 'a caw-fee" like a true New Yorker.

- Ask a local, "What's the best spot for a bagel around here?" – and follow their directions. They'll have strong opinions!

Explorer facts

- The subway system is over 120 years old. It opened in 1904 and had only one line. Now there are over 400 stations!

- Some of today's subway stations are over 10 stories underground, that's bigger than some office buildings are tall!

- And dogs are allowed on the subway, if they fit in a bag. So, some passengers find very big bags to hold their not-so-tiny dogs!

- Elephants crossed the Brooklyn Bridge! To prove the Brooklyn Bridge was safe, circus founder P.T. Barnum marched 21 elephants and 17 camels across the bridge in 1884.